WEIGHT TRAINING

PLAY·THE·GAME

WEIGHT TRAINING

Wesley Bright ·

WARD LOCK

First published in Great Britain in 1990
by Ward Lock Limited, Villiers House, 41–47 Strand,
London, WC2N 5JE, a Cassell Company

Reprinted 1991, 1992

Series editor Ian Morrison
Designed by Anita Ruddell

Illustrations by Jerry Malone

Text set in Helvetica
by August Filmsetting, Haydock, St Helens
Printed in England by Clays Ltd, St Ives plc.

British Library Cataloguing in Publication Data
Bright, Wesley
   Weight training. – (Play the game)
   1. Sports: Weight-lifting
   I. Title   II. Series
   796.4'1

   ISBN 0–7063–6858–4

Acknowledgments

The publishers wish to thank the following
organisations for supplying the pictures in this
book: Colorsport (page 29), Format Partners
(pages 2, 9, 19, 25, 53 and 78) and Harrod of
Lowestoft (pages 39 and 71).

**Frontispiece: Multi-gyms come in all shapes
and sizes, and serve to develop all muscle
groups.**

CONTENTS

FOREWORD

The 1980s has certainly become the age of the 'keep-fit fanatic'. Being aware of the rigours and strains modern-day life can put on their bodies, people have become conscious about their health and fitness.

Joggers are now pounding the street, and people are taking up a whole variety of sports as a means of keeping fit. Some are strenuous, some are not. Happily, many people are also turning to weight training as a means of keeping their bodies trim.

Like other forms of exercise or sport, it can be strenuous, or otherwise, depending upon your own personal goals. This is the beauty of weight training, you decide exactly what to do.

It is not only men who regularly visit their local gym to tone up their bodies, women frequent them as well as they seek to fight a bit of flab here, and a bit there, and to build up a general all-round level of fitness.

Many people think that the purpose of weight training is to develop big muscular bodies. Well, it can do that, but only if you want it to. The pastime offers far more than that. It offers hours of enjoyable fun, and through carefully worked out schedules, you can concentrate on developing specific parts of your body.

Play the Game: Weight Training is another in the excellent series of books designed to help the newcomer to any sport. The book gives you a good insight into the type of equipment you will come across in a gymnasium and, of course, you are shown how to use each piece of apparatus. Specimen routines are given and, if you are using weight training as a means of training for another sport, you are guided through the sort of routine you should be concentrating on.

Weight training can be hard work at times, but it has enormous advantages. And most importantly, it can be fun.

Ian Morrison
Series Editor, *Play the Game*

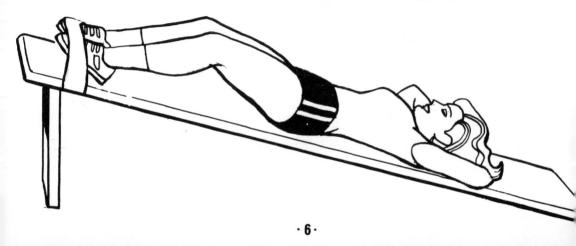

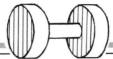

AN INTRODUCTION TO
WEIGHT
TRAINING

Many people often confuse weight training with weight-lifting. Although there is a big difference between the two, essentially the traditional weight-lifting equipment, like barbells, is used in a weight training programme.

Weight training is a means of training to develop certain parts of your body for specific purposes. Weight-lifting is an Olympic sport, and a sheer test of one's strength and power which does, of course, require weight training exercises. Here we will be concentrating only on training exercises using weights. We are not going to turn you into the next Vasiliy Alexeev.

The training and development of the body with the use of weights was first seen in Britain around the start of the 20th century. But it is only in the post-war years that sports coaches have seen weight training as a useful aid to a sportsperson's development. Athletics and swimming were the first two sports to utilize weight training techniques for its competitors but now there are very few sports which do not incorporate some form of weight training programme into their training manuals.

Weight training is designed to develop specific parts of the body. Footballers, naturally, want to develop their legs, swimmers their arms, etc. So there is a need to seek the correct advice when taking up weight training, whether it be to develop you for another sport, or just for personal enjoyment. And, of course, you must never embark on a weight training programme if there is any doubt about your health, or if you are suffering from an injury that could well be aggravated.

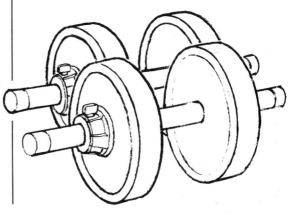

When using weight training as an aid to playing another sport, it is important that you, or your coach, fully understand what you are doing and which muscles are to be utilized. There is no sense in developing muscles that are not going to be used during the playing of your sport, or vice versa. And remember you must carry out the programme(s) correctly. Weight training can cause injury, but more often than not the blame rests with the participant and not the equipment. We will take you through **Dos and Don'ts** of weight training later. You must study them carefully.

There is plenty of weight training equipment on the market, readily available from high street sports-goods shops or from mail order catalogues. These are good value for money and you should buy according to your own budget. But you are well advised to join a local weight-training club so that you can receive sound advice from trained instructors. You can also use their wide range of equipment.

Weight training is one of those great pastimes that you can engage in on your own. And setting yourself targets you can gain personal satisfaction in reaching them. But, all too often, newcomers to weight training make the mistake of thinking they are 'better than they really are'.

If you go to a club you will see fellow members lifting, say 150 kilos, on a bench press. Whereas you may well start on something like 50–60 kilos. Don't be embarrassed. They started at exactly the same place as you. And you will find your fellow club members will encourage you in the early days of your development. So, whatever you do, **don't try to run before you can walk**. Take that advice and you will soon find you are progressing at a faster rate than you expected anyway.

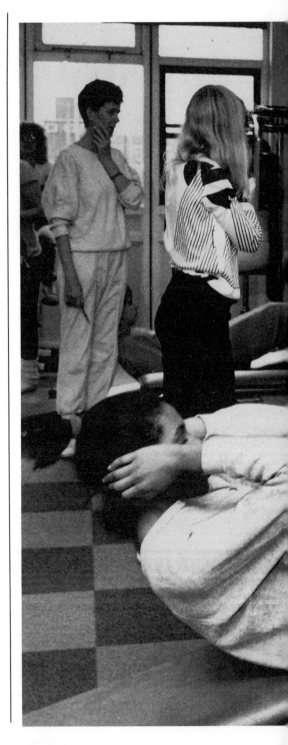

Members utilising all the equipment in the gym.

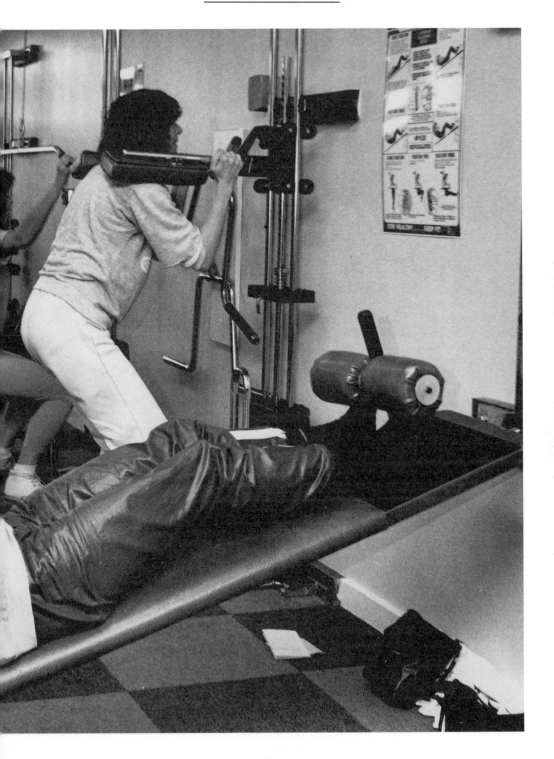

WEIGHT · TRAINING

The principle of weight training is the resistance of pressure put on you by weights. If you are finding no resistance then you are not pushing yourself enough. If you are finding the resistance too great then you are lifting weights that are too heavy for you. Both are pointless. You should gradually build up in all exercises to a point where you need maximum effort to get over that resistance. You should not start every exercise meeting resistance. You will not succeed, and will probably cause yourself some harm at the same time. Weight training is one of the safest of all physical training activities. It only becomes dangerous through negligence or stupidity.

Although we have said you must not subject yourself to excessive resistance, there is a great motto in weight training and that is: **No pain – No gain**. Write that out on a piece of paper and pin it up in your training area. Believe me, it is perhaps the most important statement we will make throughout this entire book.

It might sound a bit sadistic, but if you are without pain when weight training, you are not subjecting your body to the rigorous routine of the exercise(s).

There is no age limit on weight trainers, and there is no sexual discrimination. It is a pastime that can be enjoyed by men, women, the old, and the young. However, if you are grossly overweight, drink ten pints of beer a night, and smoke 40 cigarettes a day, don't think that by going weight training everything will be alright! It won't. You must adopt a sensible attitude to your diet and smoking and drinking habits. If you do, then you will feel a tremendous benefit from weight training. After a few weeks you will wake up in the morning feeling totally refreshed. Mind you, when you wake up the day after first taking up weight training you will hardly be able to move as a result of using previously unemployed muscles. But don't be deterred!

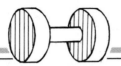

EQUIPMENT & TERMINOLOGY

Weight training equipment comes in all shapes and sizes. To get the maximum benefit from such equipment you are well advised to join a club which should have sufficient equipment to meet your needs.

However, you can easily buy such items as dumbells, barbells, multi-gyms and family fitness centres from mail order catologues, or from local sports equipment stockists. Equipment is not too expensive, but the benefit of joining a club is not only in saving on the capital outlay but in gaining the benefit of expert advice. The big problem with many people who rush out and buy a set of weights is that they don't know what to do with them once they have bought them. Advice is essential and we hope that we will be able to offer some over the following pages.

EQUIPMENT

There are two sorts of weights: fixed, and free weights. Most local authority gyms have fixed equipment. This is very safe to use (if you drop it, it won't hurt you!), but is less adaptable than free equipment which you can use in the way that suits you best. A mix of the two types of weights is ideal for any

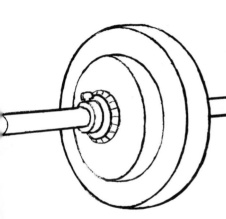

The barbell.

Note the securing nuts which must be fastened to keep the weights in place.

Weights.

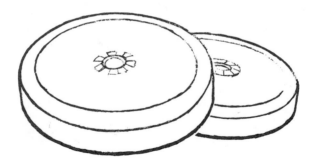

weight trainer, beginner or advanced.

Always try to use a supervized gym, rather than one which has an introductory course and then leaves you to it. It is also a good idea to have a training partner with you in the gym, to share experience and help you out if you hit a spot of trouble. You will probably push each other to train harder, too!

Let's look at the more common weight training equipment that is readily available and that which you are likely to come across in your formative stages.

Barbell

This is the classic piece of apparatus associated with weight-lifting. It is a steel bar approximately 120cm (4ft) to 210cm (7ft) long. To each end are attached weights. The weights are normally made of cast iron or steel and vary in weight and size, thus allowing for any increased weight, normally in 2.5kg stages, to be added to the bar. Some weights are made out of weighted vinyl discs.

It is important that the weights on each end of the barbell are identical, otherwise

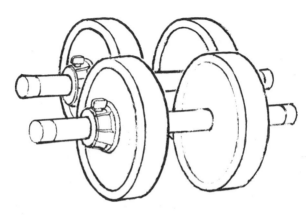

Dumbells with removable weights.

One-piece dumbells of varying weights.

accidents can occur. It is also important that the collars are tightened after the weights have been added to the bar. If not, they are likely to slip and make lifting extremely difficult and dangerous.

Dumbell

These are smaller versions of the barbell and are for holding in a single hand when carrying out exercises involving the arms.

They normally come in pairs and the weights attached to each end are not as great as those attached to the barbell. The dumbells are approximately 16in (40cm) long. They either come with separate weights which can be added or taken off as required (like the barbell), or come in one piece, and thus not capable of having extra weights added. If you buy the latter, you need to buy several sets so as to provide a variety of weights. This is where joining a weight training club

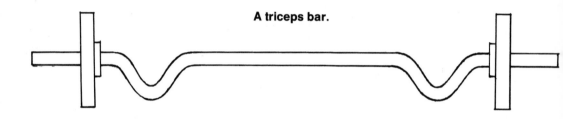

A triceps bar.

will help save you money. They will have numerous dumbell sets.

Triceps bar

Specially designed to develop the triceps. Its hold is not along the horizontal of the bar but on the two vertical support bars within the 'frame' inset into the bar. Weights are added,or taken off, to suit your individual capabilities.

Exercise bench

A tubular or rigid-framed bench used for bench pressing and other exercises. The

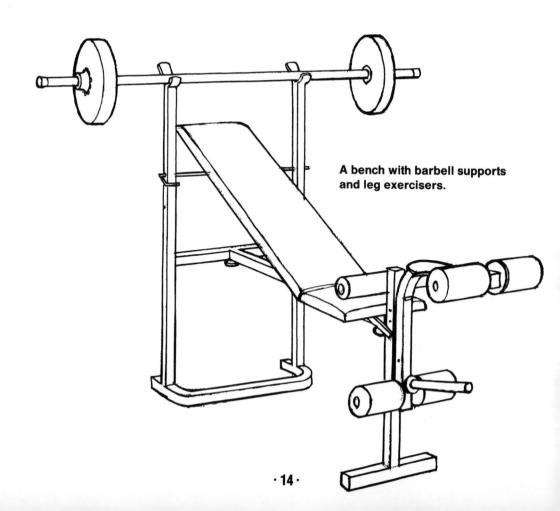

A bench with barbell supports and leg exercisers.

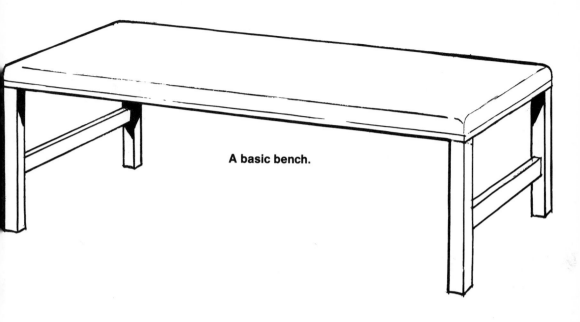

A basic bench.

bench should be padded and ideally should be adjustable to allow it to be set in an inclined position according to the exercise being carried out. Exercise benches often incorporate leg lifting units, for leg exercises, and barbell supports. Benches should not be too low or, indeed, too high. Rather, the ideal height should enable you to place the soles of your feet flat on the floor over the end of the bench when lying on your back.

Strength builder

These are ideal for developing the shoulders, chest, arms and back muscles using isometric exercises. Although not used for weight training exercises (it does not use weight), the resistance principle is nevertheless employed. It is an ideal warming-up exercise for weight training, and should be restricted to bursts of five seconds.

Multi-gym

Also called a Family Fitness Centre. As the name implies, they are designed for a multitude of exercises including lat exercises, leg curls and pulley bar exercises, amongst others. The main feature is the pulley system with adjustable weights. Time is saved in the altering of weights with the multi-gym. They can often be altered at the turn of a key or pin. And, of course, with the safety of the multi-gym, you do not need to have an accomplice to assist with your exercises as a safety precaution. Also, multi-gyms save a great deal of space that would normally be taken up by several sets of pulleys, barbells, etc.

Foodstuffs

There are a wide variety of these on the market to help you with your weight training. Calorie-rich drinks are available for those people who are using weight training as a means of increasing body weight, and meat and fibre-based protein supplements are

The strength builder.

It can be used as shown by pulling apart or by turning upside-down and pressing on the handles.

The multi-gym.

Weights are attached to the pulley system.

A more sophisticated bench with arm exercisers as well as those for the legs, and barbell supports.

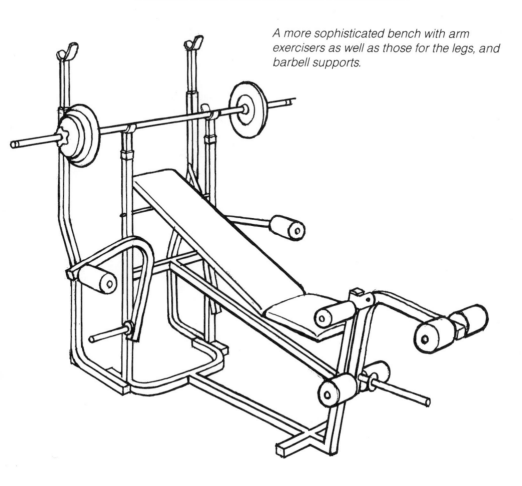

available as an aid to the muscle-building process. But you are recommended to seek advice before buying such weight training aids.

All the foregoing is the equipment you will find in your high street shop. Of course, your local weight training gym will have that lot, and probably in a more sophisticated form too. And they will have more than one set of barbells and weights, thus offering all its members plenty of choice.

The only other equipment you need worry about is clothing. There are no set guidelines but obviously you don't want to wear anything so loose fitting that it interferes with your exercise. And neither do you want to wear anything too tightly fitting that will make exercising difficult. The time of the year dictates what you wear. If it is hot, then shorts and a tee shirt are adequate. If it is cold, then a tracksuit would be ideal. Never go into a routine either too hot or too cold.

Right, now let's look at some weight-training terms and terminology.

TERMINOLOGY

The terms you will encounter refer to the actual lifts or exercises and also to parts of the body. We will look at them both separately.

The body

The following are the main muscles that we are going to be concentrating on as we look at techniques and routines later in the book.

Biceps   A general term refering to the muscles found in the arms and legs.

Cardio-vascular fitness   General fitness training for the heart and lungs which requires the heart-rate to be kept at a high level for 20–30 minutes.

Deltoids   The muscles on the cap of the shoulders.

Extensors   A general term for muscles which 'extend' a limb or part of the body.

Femoris   Muscles at the back of the upper leg.

Gastrocnemius   The calf muscle.

Gleutius   The muscle at the top of the back of the leg leading into the bottom, or posterior.

Latissimus dorsi   The muscles in the sides of the upper back.

Pectorals   The muscles at the top of the chest. Known often simply as 'Pecs'.

Quadriceps   The thigh muscle.

Improvisation with gym equipment doesn't do any harm provided you stop and think what you are doing beforehand.

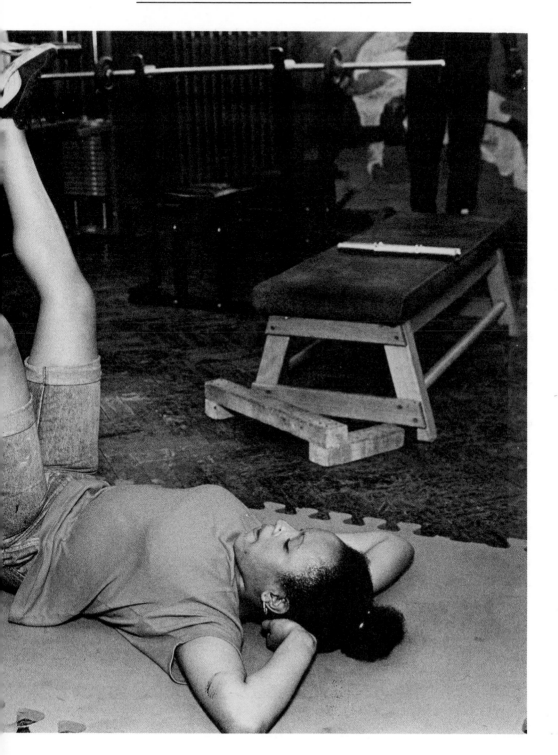

Technical terminology

Bends Any exercise that involves the bending of the trunk either sideways or forward.

Bench press One of the basic weight training techniques of lifting the barbell from your chest to an outstretched arm position while lying on a bench. Some bench presses are performed on an inclined bench. See also **Press**.

Cleans Taking the bar from floor to chest in one movement. This involves lifting the barbell from the floor starting with your knees bent, and back flat, grasping the bar just outside shoulder width. Extend the legs, pushing the chest up, bending the arms, and rising onto your toes. As the bar reaches the top of the chest, your wrists are turned over, the knees bent, and heels returned to the floor. This is one of the standard lifts in weight-lifting.

Curls An exercise using the arms. Curls can be two-handed and using a barbell, or single-handed using either one, or two, dumbells. The exercises are carried out by holding the weight in your hand and curling it towards your chest by bending the arms at the elbow, keeping the bar close to the body at all times.

Dead lift So called because you are, in effect, lifting a dead weight. The bar is placed in front of the feet, and lifted in one movement to the front of the thighs. It is an excellent exercise for strengthening the spine, and one of the three competitive power lifts.

Trapezius Muscles from the side of the neck leading down the centre of the back, and towards the shoulder.

Triceps Muscles leading from the back of the upper arm to across the elbow joint.

Forward raise A dumbell exercise in which two dumbells (one in each hand) are raised from a relaxed position near your thighs to an outstretched position in front of you and level with your shoulders. It can be carried out by raising both dumbells simultaneously or alternately.

The 'dead lift'. The barbell is lowered to the ground in a controlled manner. Keep the arms straight and bend from the waist.

Lateral raise   Another dumbell exercise. This time the dumbells are lifted to the side by outstretching the arms. A lateral raise can be carried out by standing upright, with the trunk bent forwards, or by lying on a bench. Both are equally valuable.

Lunges   A form of squat, lunges are carried out with the barbell held in a position across your chest or behind your neck. Position one leg in front of the other and lunge forward by bending your knees. It is an ideal exercise for strengthening the legs.

Press   The press is the action of lifting the barbell from a chest position to a position above the head with arms outstretched. See also **Bench press**.

Pull-over An exercise carried out on the bench and using either a barbell, triceps bar or adjustable dumbell with a single weight in the middle so that you can grip both ends of the bar. The weight is taken from a starting position on the chest, lifted over the head and moved out of sight behind it. The pull-over can be done with the arms bent (starting on the chest), or straight (starting vertically above the chest).

Pull-up So called because the barbell is pulled up towards the chin. It can either be a high pull-up whereby the bar is pulled from the floor to the chin, or a half pull-up, when it is started at knee-height and pulled upwards, again to the chin. This is a good exercise for developing a weak back, and if only light

weights are used, is a good exercise for warming up with.

Pyramid system A system of training whereby the number of repetitions is gradually reduced until one maximum lift is attained. This type of exercise is often carried out during the winter schedule.

Repetitions Generally abbreviated to *reps*. Weight training, unlike weight-lifting, does not work on the principle of being able to successfully make one lift. The key to its success lies in the fact that exercises are being performed in a series of repetitions. For example, you may set yourself a schedule of ten lifts of the barbell at a specific weight. Those ten lifts are called repetitions. The number of repetitions depends upon whether you want to develop general cardio-vascular fitness. If that is the case then a high number of repetitions with lower weights should be employed. If you want to develop strength and power then the number of repetitions is reduced but the weight is increased.

Resistance One of the basic principles of weight training is being able to resist weight by the various exercises. There is no sense in comfortably lifting a barbell for 10, 20 or 30 repetitions without getting a sweat on. That will do you no good. You have to work a programme which will offer you a challenge and you must be able to *resist* and overcome that challenge.

Rowing The action of this exercise is, as its name implies, a rowing one. It can either be carried out by using both hands and the barbell, or by using single hands, each with a dumbell.

Sequence method A popular form of training which offers great variety. You do a complete 'tour' of the gym, completing one set of, say, ten repetitions on each piece of apparatus before moving on the next one, and so on, before repeating the routine.

Sets Weight training programmes are so designed that you perform your repetitions in sets. For example, you may do ten bench presses as one set, but your whole routine may incorporate three sets. In other words you will eventually do 30 presses.

Squats The bending of your legs from an upright position into a 'seated' position with the barbell either behind your neck or on the chest. An excellent exercise for developing leg and back muscles.

Triceps press Exercise to develop the triceps and carried out with two dumbells. Can either be effected from a standing position or on a bench.

Before going on to the actual exercises, we should now look at some of the uses of weight-training, particularly if you are using the training as an aid to another sport.

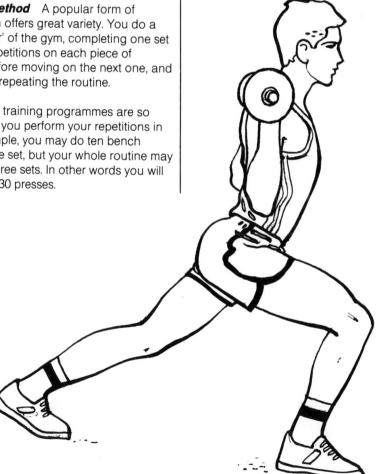

WEIGHT TRAINING –

ITS USES

You may have decided you want to take up weight training for a variety of reasons: you may feel that you are overweight; you may feel you are getting no other form of exercise; you may want to exercise a limb or limbs as part of a recuperation process following an accident or operation, or you may want to take it up as an aid to another activity or sport. No matter which category you fall into, weight training has something to offer. The benefits are great and so is the enjoyment, provided you enter into the activity with the right attitude.

The first thing you must remember is **it takes time**. Don't be impatient and get frustrated because other people are lifting heavier weights than you. We have already stated this point, but it is an important one. Everybody started at the same place as you at some time. Never forget that.

OK, so what exactly can weight training do for you?

As a sportsperson it will help develop power and offer a general increase in fitness. It will also prove beneficial to you when you take part in other training programmes that, say, your swimming coach will have designed for you. And, of course, weight training strengthens your muscles and ligaments, thus reducing the risks of injury and at the same time helping to strengthen those muscles that may have been weakened or damaged in the past.

Specific exercises are also designed to cater for those individuals who need to concentrate on speed and/or endurance, and this is where it is important to look at all the exercises available and decide just what you want them for. It is no good spending most of your time in the gym developing your leg muscles if you are a javelin thrower. Yes, leg exercises would be

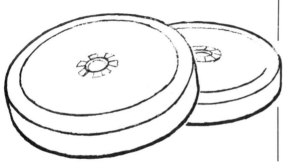

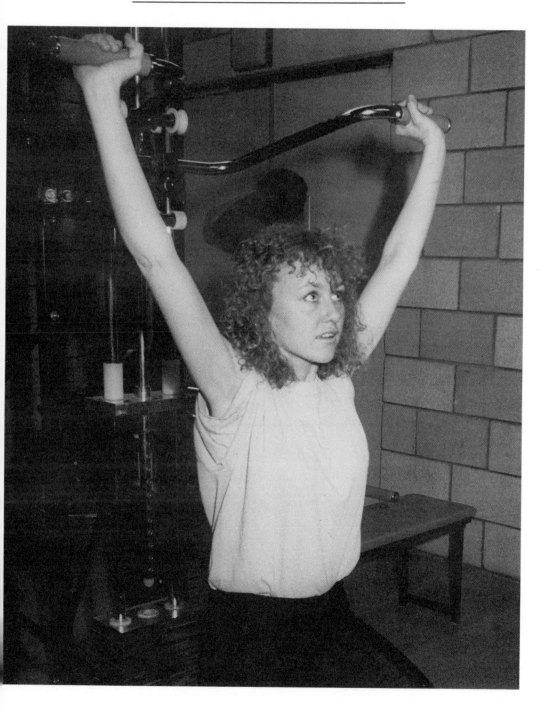

Weight training isn't just for men.

considered in this case, but the emphasis must be on the arms. It is therefore crucial if you are a competitive sportsperson to seek professional advice as to the sort of schedule that is needed for your own demands. It must be remembered, however, that weight training in only an aid to your sport. It won't make you a better swimmer or tennis player. But it will help towards your fitness, stamina, etc.

If you are taking up weight training for general fitness, and not allying it to another sport, then you can consider carrying out all of the exercises shown on the following pages, but only do the ones you enjoy. Bear in mind, however, that if you restrict your choice of exercises too much, you will become over-developed in some muscles, and under-developed in others. Remember our motto: **No pain – no gain**.

It is important that you assess your purpose for weight training. If it is for general fitness, then you will be aiming to develop a programme that incorporates many repetitions, but with lighter weights. On saying that, the word 'lighter' in this case means the weights which you can lift for 10–20 repetitions with resistance towards the end of the reps. It is no good feeling resistance after 2–3 reps because you are doing yourself no good, and are not likely to benefit. For general fitness, the key is: **more repetitions at lighter weights**.

If you are using weight training to develop your powers of endurance, say for long distance swimming, then you should lift even lighter weights, and increase the repetitions in the 8–30 range with little rest in between sets and/or exercises.

On the other hand, if you are using weight training to develop strength, then the number of repetitions is reduced considerably to 3–8 repetitions, but the weights are increased substantially.

It is also important that you assess your training pattern according to the time of the year. For general fitness, the 'season' can be divided into a summer and winter schedule. In the latter, you will be looking at increasing weights and reducing repetitions as you develop more strength and stamina after a summer of general exercises.

However, if, for example, you are a footballer, you will have to control your weight training according to the time of the year. Emphasis should be on all-round fitness in the close season with as many different exercises as possible being employed, each with heavy weights, but in reduced sets, say two sets of 10–15 reps each. As the season approaches, the exercises relevant to the particular sport should receive greater emphasis and the number of sets be increased, but so too should the weights. This should be stepped up after a couple of weeks to coincide with the start of the season. Finally, once the season is under way, this level of power should be maintained by reducing the repetitions but increasing the number of sets and maintaining, or slightly increasing, the weights.

This multi-gym exercise is to develop the leg muscles.

EXERCISES & TECHNIQUES

Being able to lift weights is one thing, but being able to lift them properly is another. A good technique is crucial to successful weight training. Furthermore, a bad technique can cause injury. So, right at the outset, concentrate on this aspect. The lifting of heavier weights will instinctively come if you have a good technique.

When you first take hold of the barbell to do your first bench press, you will find it a strange feeling and, despite the weight being minimal, you will have difficulty in lifting and

lowering the barbell in a straight line. But once you have mastered that, then you will be amazed at how quickly you will make progress.

We have already mentioned the need to plan your weight-training schedule. If you are training as an aid to another sport then seek advice as to what areas you should be concentrating on. However, if you are training as a general fitness enthusiast, work your way around all the pieces of apparatus in the gym and get used to them all. Spend your first few visits familiarizing yourself with them and after a couple of weeks decide upon a programme to suit yourself, and incorporate those pieces of equipment that you feel most comfortable with into your routine.

As you know, the basis of weight training is **resistance**, but it takes a while to assess the amount of resistance you can withstand. This, of course, starts to form a pattern once you have mastered techniques. After about 3–4 weeks, you should be getting some idea of the resistance you can withstand and you will then be ready to work out a programme. We will show you a typical programme for a beginner at the end of this chapter. It is pointless trying to work one out until you can realistically assess your 'starting point'.

Unfortunately, we cannot tell you at what weight you should start any specific exercise.

All of us are built differently. Consequently, our capabilities vary. You must remember when selecting your starting point that you are going to build up to 10, or even 20 repetitions. So, while a weight may feel nice and light on repetition number one, just stop and think what it is going to feel like 19 repetitions later!

We are going to look at exercises using both free weights – barbells, dumbells, etc – and those using weight-training machines (fixed apparatus) like the multi-gym. The former category is probably the one you are most likely to use because free weights are readily available. Before looking at the exercises, however, there are a couple of points that need covering.

Sets and repetitions

These have already cropped up several times on the previous pages and we are going to clarify them a bit further here, because they are so important.

When weight training, you don't pick up a pair of dumbells and exercise with them for, say, five minutes, and then move on to a barbell and do curls for, say, two minutes. Weight training is more organized than that.

You must have a clear picture what you are going to do the moment you walk into the gym.

Having decided your 'starting point', as outlined on the previous pages, you now decide how many lifts you can do of, say, 40 kilos. If the answer is 10, then you must do 10 lifts at 40 kilos. These are known as 10 repetitions. But don't restrict it to one set of 10 reps, plan your schedule to do, say, three sets. In other words you are lifting the barbell 30 times, but in three sets of 10. All exercises should be done in sets.

For general fitness you should not increase your number of sets from three, but you can, with experience and development, increase the number of repetitions from 10 to 15 and then from 15 to 20. As time goes by, you will be constantly increasing the weights lifted.

Breathing

It is crucial that you breath properly. Fill your lungs full of air before each lift and, as a rule, breath out while completing it. So, it's generally breath in on the effort, and breath out after the effort.

Warming up

Before starting your programme it is essential that you carry out some warming-up exercises. It is important that you don't go into a programme with cold muscles.

The form a warming-up routine takes depends on your own personal choice. Many people go through a 'mini' routine using very light weights, or simply do on-the-spot exercises making sure the arms and legs are well limbered up. But for a good 'loosener', and one that will shake away the cobwebs, you want to try sit-ups either on the floor or on an inclined board.

With your feet supported, knees bent

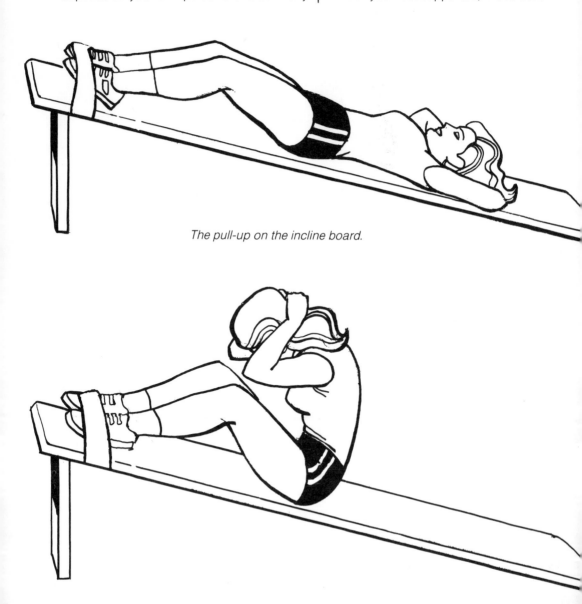

The pull-up on the incline board.

The power clean lift of the barbells from the floor to the chest.

slightly, and your hands behind your head, pull yourself up so that your head touches your knees. Do this for ten repetitions and in three sets with a one-minute breather in between. For variety, alternate touching your knees with first your left elbow and then your right. Don't forget, when they become easy, increase the repetitions to 15 or more, and so on.

This is a good exercise for also winding down at the end of a weight-training schedule. You will be surprised how many repetitions you can do at the end of your programme. Invariably it will be more than you could manage at the start.

Recommended programme for the novice

The first exercises we are going to look at are five exercises with free weights which are ideal for the beginner. They are so designed

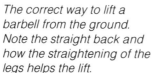

The correct way to lift a barbell from the ground. Note the straight back and how the straightening of the legs helps the lift.

to provide benefit to all muscle groups in the body and they are in a pre-determined order to enable each muscle group to recover in time before the next exercise.

And don't forget, if you are training for stamina then more repetitions (up to 30) at lighter weights are required. If you are training for strength development then the weights should be heavy enough to keep the repetitions at ten or below.

First, though, you must learn how to lift weights correctly, to avoid injury. The 'Power Clean' is the basic lifting technique which is an excellent exercise in its own right and forms the foundation of lifting weights for weight training. The aim is to lift the bar from

your head in line with the rest of your body. Finally, push upwards with your hands and turn your wrists so that the palms support the bar at the top of the lift. When you return the barbell to the start position this should be with a controlled movement rather than it being 'dropped'.

The power clean is a great all-round power builder, particularly in the development of the quadriceps, gleutius, and the back muscles, and it is used by sports people in many different fields. Because it uses many smaller muscles, it is a popular exercise for general all-round fitness.

An adaption is the power curl which is carried out in the same way except the palms face outwards when holding the bar.

Right, that's that out of the way, now on to the exercises.

Exercise one–*Press (behind the neck)*
From a starting position, hold the barbell across the shoulders and spread your hands wider than shoulder width.

Your back should be straight and legs slightly apart at hip width. Push upwards on the bar until your arms are outstretched. Bring the bar back to its start position under control and then repeat without stopping. When the bar is lowered from its upright position, make sure to bring it down slowly on to your neck and shoulders. Don't pull it down too violently... it might hurt!

This exercise helps to develop those muscles in the upper back, the shoulder, and those at the back of the arm.

floor to chest in one continuous movement.

The starting position should be a crouched one, with feet placed under the bar at hip width, and your back flat. Your hips should be higher than your knees, and the bar is held by hands at shoulder width. The lift is done by straightening your body, keeping the back and arms straight and

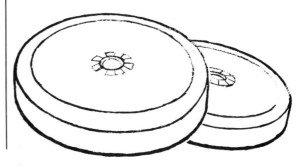

WEIGHT · TRAINING

The behind-the-neck press from behind.

When bench pressing, make sure you have an accomplice to assist.

Exercise two–*Bench press*

It is important that you have an assistant to help you with this exercise to help lift the barbell from its stand into your hands, and back to the stand after the completion of your repetitions. Don't forget, there will be a time when you cannot manage your reps so it is crucial to have assistance.

Lie on the bench with your head at, but not over, the end. Get into a comfortable position with your feet flat on the ground. Don't ask for the bar to be placed into your hands until you are absolutely ready.

Once you have taken the bar, rest it on your chest and from that position push it upwards while straightening your arms at the same time. Gently return the bar to your chest and repeat. Make sure your hands are fairly wide apart on the bar.

This exercise develops the chest muscles (pectoralis), those at the back of the upper arm (the extensors), and the front shoulder muscles (flexors). If you want to develop the triceps more than the pectorals the best way to do this is by holding the bar with your hands closer together.

The bench press.

From a position with the bar across your chest...
...lift it straight up into the air.

Bench pressing is one of the basic lifts in weight training.

Correct breathing is crucial with bench pressing. It will help towards making a good technique. If you get the technique wrong on this exercise you can expect all sorts of problems. One of the biggest faults of the novice, apart from not breathing properly, is returning the barbell too quickly to its start position. It is not necessary to carry out this exercise with great speed.

If you are doing this exercise properly, and have selected a suitable starting weight, you will find resistance on approximately the 8th repetition on the first set. On the second set you will find resistance at about 6–7 and on the third set it will start at about the 5th or 6th repetition.

Bench pressing is an ideal exercise for those sportspeople who need to develop their upper trunk, like shot-putters, javelin throwers, discus throwers, etc.

The two-handed barbell curl with palms facing outwards.

... and with palms facing inwards.

Exercise three—*Two-handed barbell curl*
After the last exercise your arms are going to
be tired. Give them a short breather before
going into this next exercise, the two-handed
curl with the barbell.

With your arms by your side and body
upright, hold the barbell in front of you with
your palms facing forward. To carry out the
curl bend your arms at the elbow but make
sure the barbell is kept close to your body as
you raise it to your chest.

This exercise is designed to develop those
muscles in the front of your upper arm (arm
flexors), and is one you would spend time
practising if you were a devotee of gymnastics.

Bent forward rowing. Note that only the arms
and barbell move.

The view from the side.

The squat with the barbell behind the neck. Don't squat down too far.

Exercise four–*Bent forward rowing*

With the knees slightly bent and back kept firm and straight, hold the barbell with outstretched arms at a height of approximately 30cm (12in) from the ground. Keeping your head up and back firm and straight, pull the barbell up to your chest by bending the arms and pushing your elbows out to the side of your body. Return to the original position and repeat. Your trunk does not move during the exercise, only the arms.

It is ideal for developing the upper back muscles and is an exercise that rowers would take advantage of. Also, archery and shooting competitors might use this exercise as a means of improving their shoulder posture, something that is very important in both sports.

Exercise five–*Squat*

A perfect exercise for track athletes, or any sportsperson who uses his/her legs as his/her

The squat with the barbell on top of the chest.

main source of power.

The squat is an excellent exercise for the cardio-vascular system in general, if performed with light weights and high repetition. It can be performed with the barbell either behind the neck or (for beginners especially) resting on the top of the chest.

Whichever you chose, make sure your feet are a comfortable distance apart. The lift is carried out by squatting down towards the floor but, as you reach the lower level (without

touching the floor) you should return to the upright position pulling yourself up with your head and straightening your legs. Don't go too far down in the squat position, you may not get up.

The squat is a good exercise for those people who want to increase their weight because it uses so many different muscle groups.

To the novice, the squat is quite difficult to control as confidence is needed to go all the

The half-squat with the barbell behind the neck.

way down into the squat position. Keep at it. If the achilles tendons are tight, place a piece of wood, approximately 2.3–3cm (1–1½in) thick, underneath your heels. This will keep them on something solid until the achilles tendons stretch, and so help maintain your balance.

If you decide on the front squat (with the barbell on your chest), as opposed to it being on the back of the neck, then it should be effected in the same way but you are now putting greater emphasis on your thigh and hip muscles.

As a variation, you can turn the squat into a squat jump. This time, however, don't go into the full squat position. Adopt a 'half-squat' and from there jump forwards. But make sure you flex your knees on landing to take the weight out of the jump. This adaptation helps develop the leg and thigh muscles. This exercise is invaluable to the long distance runner as it builds stamina and cardio-vascular endurance.

The half-squat with the barbell on the top of the chest.

FURTHER · EXERCISES

You will have noticed that so far all exercises have been with barbells. We will shortly be looking at those using dumbells and other equipment, but first, let's look at other barbell exercises.

Pull-up Also known as the High pull-up, it is so-named because the bar is pulled up from a low starting position to a point close in front of your chin, beginning with the 'get set' position.

As you straighten your legs, lift the bar upwards by bending your elbows outwards. At the top of the pull, your upper arms and elbows should be parallel with the bar, your body upright, and on your toes.

The exercise is often used as a warming-up exercise with light weights. But with heavier weights it is a good exercise for developing all-round power.

The pull-up
Note how the upper arms are parallel with the bar at the top of the pull.

Upright rowing The action is not dissimilar to the pull-up, but this time the bar is held with both hands near to its middle and the starting position is upright. The body doesn't move throughout the movement, only the hands and arms, which pull the bar up to your chin. At the top of the action your hands should be lower than your elbows. Lower the bar gently to the start position, and repeat. This is a good exercise for the shoulder abductors.

Upright rowing.

Note the position of the hands and elbows at the top of the pull.

The press – one of the lifts used in weight-lifting. Note how the entire body, including arms, is straight.

Press from chest   From a start position with the bar across your chest, lift it above your head by straightening your arms. Your palms should be facing outwards.

   This exercise should be performed either standing with your legs slightly apart (at hip width) although advanced people may do it sitting on a bench.

   An excellent variation of this lift is from the seated position. Start with the bar resting on your chest and lift it so that on alternate 'down' movements it alternates between coming to rest behind your neck and on your chest.

The lunge with barbell behind the neck.

Lunge The lunge is an exercise carried out by squash, badminton and tennis players because it develops mobility in the legs, crucial to all those sports.

The start position is an upright stance with one leg ahead of the other and the barbell is held across the chest with palms facing outwards. From that position, lunge forward by bending your knees. The front knee should end up ahead of the front foot and the rear knee remains straight. You should make sure you have got your balance before attempting the lunge.

After returning to the start position you must alternate your leading foot. The lunge can also be carried out with the barbell behind the neck.

Trunk forward bend Similar to the squat, except this time the trunk is bent forward as opposed to the knees being bent.

Assume a start position as for the squat with the barbell across your neck, with your hands a good distance apart and your palms facing outwards. Keep your back flat and bend forward from the hip, taking any strain off the

EXERCISES · & · TECHNIQUES

The lunge with barbell across the top of the chest.

If, at first, you don't feel confident enough to lunge with the barbell, practice with dumbells.

hamstrings by slightly bending your knees.
For developing those muscles in your lower back and those around the buttocks, the trunk forward bend is a perfect exercise.

The trunk forward bend.

You can see from this picture how the exercise is developing the arm muscles.

It's now time to get away from the barbell and look at some exercises with the **dumbells.**

Dumbell press   Start with the dumbells at shoulder-height with elbows bent. Stretch the arms upwards simultaneously, making sure they remain parallel. At the top of the lift the body should be stretched upwards as a result of lifting the chest.

The shoulder, upper back and upper arm muscles all benefit from the dumbell press. It can be carried out either standing or sitting and for variety you can lift your right arm and then the left arm alternately, and vice versa.

The dumbell press.

It can be carried out by raising both dumbells simultaneously...

...or one at a time.

The dumbell curl which can again be carried out by curling both dumbells at the same time...

...or one at a time.

Dumbell curl   The dumbell curl is the perfect exercise for developing the muscles in the front of the upper arm and is an exercise that the likes of rowers might concentrate on.

Adopt an upright position with arms hanging relaxed by your side, holding the dumbells, of course! Curl the dumbells upwards by bending your elbow and turning your hand and dumbell in towards your neck. The move can be carried out by lifting both dumbells simultaneously or by lifting first the right, then the left. For the advanced weight trainer, the exercise can also be carried out on an inclined bench.

WEIGHT · TRAINING

The lateral lift from the upright position.

Lateral lift   This exercise can be done by either standing upright (for the deltoids) or with the trunk bent forward (for the posterior deltoid). The latter is more strenuous.

If upright, start by holding the dumbells near to your thighs. From there, raise your arms to the side and lift the chest at the same time. If you carry out the exercise from the bent forward position, start with your legs slightly apart, back flat and bent forward with the dumbells held in your straight arms at a start position. From there keep the body bent forward and slowly lift the dumbells out sideways.

All lateral lifts are designed primarily for shoulder development.

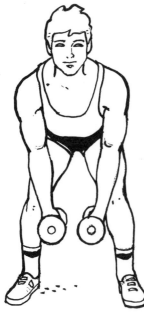

The lateral lift from the bent forward position.

WEIGHT · TRAINING

Forward raise From a start position the same as that for the upright lateral lift, raise your arms but this time the outstretched arm should be in front of you and not to the side, and to a height slightly above the shoulders. You can either raise both arms at the same time, or alternately. It is a good exercise for developing the muscles in the forearm and the front of the shoulders.

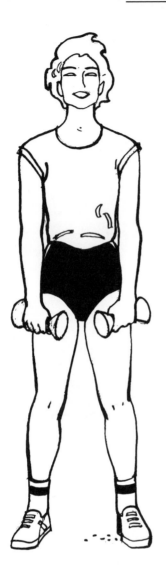

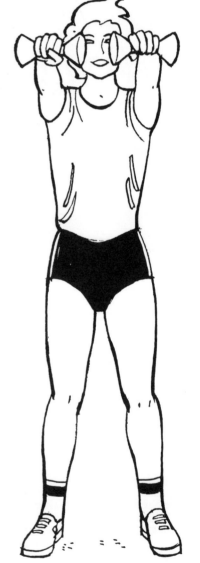

The forward raise which, like many dumbell exercises, can be done by raising the two dumbells together or one at a time.

Two exercises with the **triceps bar**:

Straight-arm pull-over A great exercise for stretching the abdominal muscles and rib cage, it also develops the muscles at the top of your arm and in the chest and small of the back.

Assume a position on the bench, not with your head over the end. Fix your eyes on a

The straight-arm pull-over.

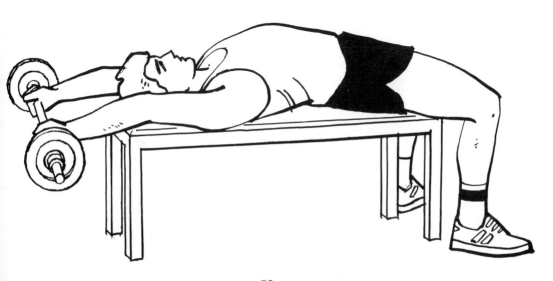

point where the wall and ceiling meet. Hold the bar with arms upright and above your chest. Gently lower the bar over your head with arms straight and your eyes fixed on the point as already mentioned. As soon as the bar has gone out of sight pull it back to its start position. Don't allow the bar to go too far over your head otherwise it will 'bounce' back to its start position and the exercise will not be made with a controlled movement. You will therefore lose the resistance of the exercise.

Bent-arm pull-over Take up a similar position on the bench as for the straight-arm pull-over, but this time with the head over the end, and again fix your eyes on the spot where

The bent-arm pull-over.

the wall and ceiling meet. The start position this time is with the bar on your chest. The bar is lifted over your head until it goes out of sight and is returned to its start position. It is important that you keep your shoulders tucked into your side and keep the bar as close to your head throughout the whole movement which should, again, be controlled.

These two pull-overs can also be carried out by using a barbell or a dumbell loaded with the weight(s) in the centre so that you can grip the bar on either side of the weight(s).

USING THE MULTI-GYM

The multi-gym offers nothing over and above the exercises already shown, but it does allow you to carry out most of the aforementioned exercises within a confined space and without the aid of an accomplice.
  With a basic multi-gym you can utilize its facilities to carry out the likes of the bench press, inclined bench press, upright rowing and squat exercises by using the weights and bars built into the machine. It is

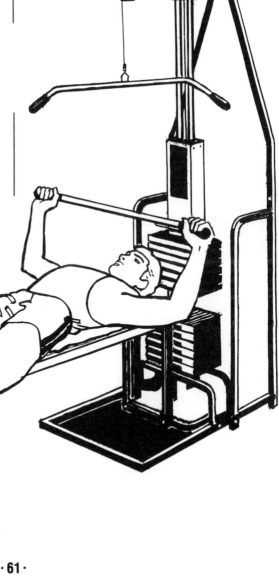

Bench pressing using the multi-gym.

The inclined bench press with the multi-gym.

Upright rowing with the multi-gym.

particularly useful for the bench press because you don't need an accomplice to standby and help you with the lifting of the bar.

But there are other exercises that the multi-gym can provide which free weights cannot. Some of these include:

The **military press**, is a very strict standing press from the chest, which can be done seated. It is a good exercise for the deltoids and triceps.

The **double leg extension** is carried out by using the leg exercisers at the end of the bench. Most good benches have these without going to the expense of buying a complete multi-gym. And such a bench is recommended if you are concentrating only on your quadriceps.

The **triceps pulldown** is, as its name implies, to benefit the triceps. It is carried out in a standing position with elbows bent and held in

The squat with the multi-gym.

Using the multi-gym for the military press.

The double leg extension can either be done on a multi-gym or on a bench fitted with leg extensions and attaching weights.

The triceps pull-down.

The 'behind-the-neck' lat pull.

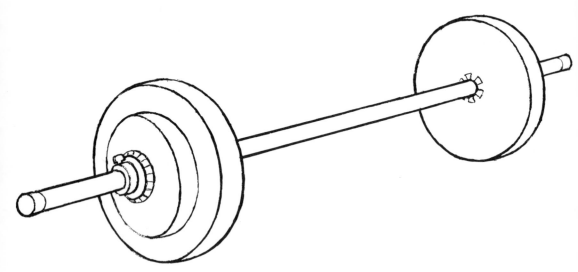

close to your side. You must control the bar, which is connected to the weighted pulley, by holding it at the start position (waist high) and letting it rise to chest height before returning it to its original position. It must be carried out with a controlled movement so as to apply more resistance on the triceps.

The *lat pull (behind-the-neck)* is another exercise using the weighted pulley system. This time you sit with your back to the lat bar and pull the bar downwards to a position behind your neck. It must again be a controlled exercise otherwise the benefits to your deltoids and biceps will be reduced.

If you have access to a lat bar or multi-gym, these last two exercises are good ones to be carried out before you do your bench presses because they get your biceps and triceps warmed up and ready to cope with the weights that the bench press has to offer.

We have now covered most of the major exercises that you are likely to encounter, or want to experiment with, as a newcomer to weight training. There are, of course, many more, but they are for a later stage in your development. Remember; **don't run before you can walk.**

In certain cases we have tried to indicate which exercises are of particular benefit to certain sports. It should be quite straightforward to identify which exercises will be of benefit to you if you are using weight training for a particular sport. Most people, however, will probably be using weight training as a means of general fitness and we said earlier that we would draw up a programme for you to work to.

The following is to be followed purely as a guideline. We cannot decide what starting weight you should choose. As we have said, only you can determine that after a couple of weeks in the gym. But once you have decided

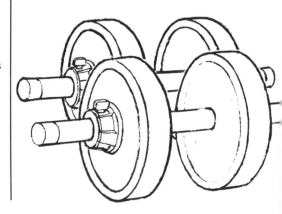

on your starting weight, which we will call x for the purpose of designing your programme, you can them insert your own figures as a replacement for x. A nominal weight of, say, 10 kg would be a good starting point.

Remember, that this programme should be adapted to suit your own personal needs and preferences. You may not like some of the exercises included. OK, change them and replace them with the ones you enjoy doing.

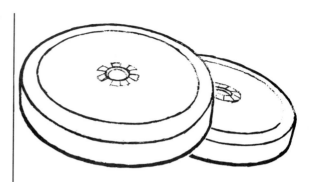

Warming up

(a) 2 minutes general loosening up exercises, swinging arms, etc.

(b) Sit-ups on an inclined board. 3 sets of 10 repetitions. Increase this to 3 sets of 15 repetitions after a few weeks by building up as follows:
Week 2:   2 sets of 10, 1 set of 15
Week 3:   1 set of 10, 2 sets of 15
Week 4:   3 sets of 15
You can continue to build it up in a similar fashion if you so desire, but don't forget, it is only a warming-up exercise and 3 sets of 15 should be plenty to loosen you up. In winter, you should ensure your warm-up is longer to guard against injury.

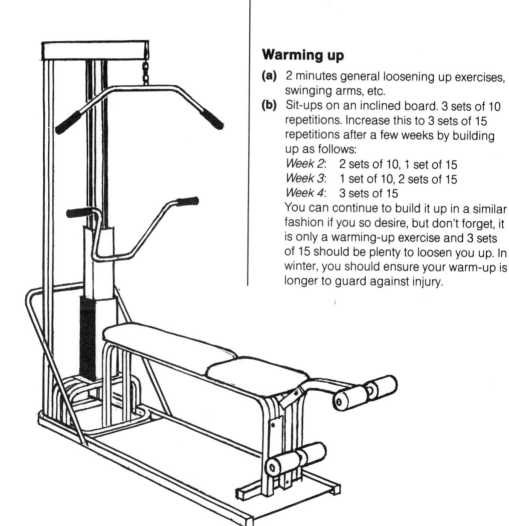

(c) The triceps pull-down.

(d) The 'behind-the-neck' lat pull.

(e) The bench press.

(f) The behind-the-neck press.

Lat Bar (if available)

(c) Triceps pull-down
(d) Lat pull (behind-the-neck)
For these two exercises follow this routine:

Summer:
Week 1: 3 sets of 10 at weight ×
Week 2: 2 sets of 10, 1 set of 15 at ×
Week 3: 1 set of 10, 2 sets of 15 at ×
Week 4: 3 sets of 15 at ×

Week 5: 2 sets of 15, 1 set of 20 at ×
Week 6: 1 set of 15, 2 sets of 20 at ×
Week 7: 3 sets of 20 at ×

Winter:
Restrict repetitions to 10 but increase sets
to 4 and increase weights each week as
per the bench press summer example
below.

(e) Bench press

Summer:
Week 1: 3 sets of 10 at weight ×
Week 2: 2 sets of 10 at ×, 1 set of 10 at
× +5 kg
Week 3: 1 set of 10 at ×, 2 sets of 10 at
× +5 kg
Week 4: 3 sets of 10 at × +5 kg
Week 5: 2 sets of 10 at × +5 kg, 1 set of
10 at × +10 kg
Week 6: 1 set of 10 at × +5 kg, 2 sets of
10 at × +10 kg
Week 7: 3 sets of 10 at × +10 kg
and so on...

Winter:
Take your maximum finishing weight from
the summer schedule, and use this figure
as × in the following repetitions.
7 lifts at × minus 20 kg
6 lifts at × minus 15 kg
5 lifts at × minus 10 kg
4 lifts at × minus 5 kg
3 lifts at ×
2 lifts at × plus 5 kg
1 lift at × plus 10 kg
This is called the pyramid system, and
sets a goal weight for strength of 5 kg
above your maximum weight. You do **not**
repeat the pyramid system over 3 sets. It
constitutes the equivalent of 3 sets.
Increase your starting weight by 5 kg each
week.

(g) The barbell curl.

(h) The dumbell lateral raise.

(f) Behind-the-neck press
(g) Barbell curl
(h) Dumbell lateral raise (bending)
(i) Dumbell curl (standing)
(j) Dumbell forward raise
(k) Straight-arm pull-over
(l) Bent-arm pull-over

All the above exercises (f) to (l) should be carried out in the same way as the lat exercises. That applies to both the summer and winter schedules.

(m) ...and finally, why don't you 'wind-down' by doing some more pull-ups on the inclined board? Try to do as many as you can. It's a tiring, but satisfying way to finish your programme.

(i) The dumbell curl.

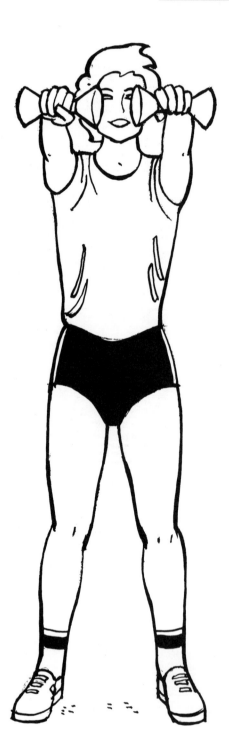

(j) The dumbell forward raise.

The exercises as outlined should be carried out in that order but in groups as follows:
- (a) and (b)
- (c) and (d)
- (e)
- (f) and (g)
- (h), (i) and (j)
- (k) and (l)
- (m)

Don't move on to the next group until you have finished one group. When doing a group with more than one exercise in, carry out set 1 of the first exercise, move to set 1 of the next and then return to the first exercise, and so on, until all sets are completed in that group.

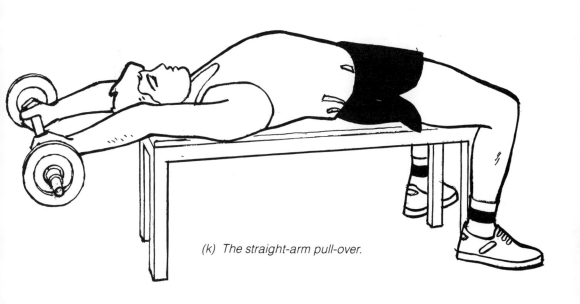

(k) The straight-arm pull-over.

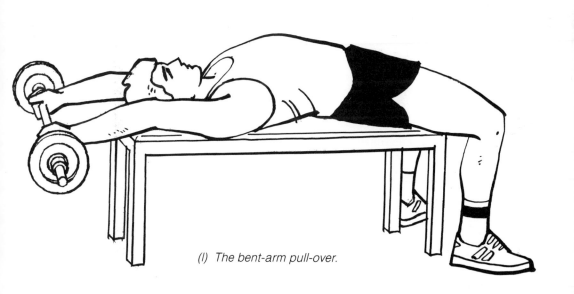

(l) The bent-arm pull-over.

WEIGHT TRAINING
CLINIC

Having now introduced some of the basic weight training routines and exercises, there may be some points about which you are not quite clear. Hopefully, the weight training clinic will clear up those unanswered points. So here goes:

Why do we do exercises in sets?

Because weight training is a gradual development. Carrying out exercises in repetitions and sets helps that development process by encouraging blood to flow through the areas being worked.

Is it necessary to always have somebody helping me with my exercises?

Not always. For example, you wouldn't require anybody to help you when working with dumbells, or if you were using a multi-gym. However, it is imperative when lifting heavy weights with the barbell, either doing presses, curls, or squats, that you have somebody in attendance. It is particularly important when you are bench pressing because you need somebody to lift the weights off the supports and into your hands. You could probably do that yourself but try to put them back after pushing yourself to the limit on ten repetitions. You don't need to be told how dangerous it could be if the barbell slipped out of your hands and on to your windpipe.

Whoever is helping you with any exercise must fully understand what you are doing and how many repetitions you are carrying out. It is also important that he/she doesn't just pick up the bar and drop it into your hand. They must be aware of when you are ready to take it and must only release their grip on a signal from you. When supporting the bar for somebody carrying out a bench press you must always have one hand under the bar and one over, as shown in the diagram. This gives extra support in case it slips.

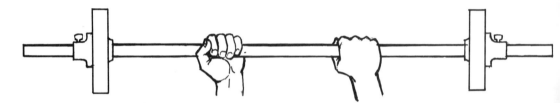

When passing the barbell to somebody, or carrying it, do so with one hand over the bar, and one under it.

Benches often come fitted with arm exercisers, and leg exercisers. They are not just for bench pressing.

How long should I rest or pause in between sets or exercises?

That depends on the type of training you are doing. But in the normal course of fitness training you should, as a guideline, keep it to a minimum and just long enough to get your normal breath back. This normally takes about one minute. In between exercises you should take a couple of deep breaths and keep the arms and legs moving. If you rest for longer periods, the benefit to the cardio-vascular system will be reduced.

How many times a week should I train

Again, this depends on what you are training for. But as a guideline three times a week with at least a day's rest in between is ideal.

How long should a schedule last for?

You're going to ask how long is a piece of string next I can tell! Again, it depends on the type of training you are doing. It also depends on how many other people are in the gym at the same time wanting to use the same piece(s) of apparatus. As a guideline, anything between 30–60 minutes should be sufficient. If only 30 minutes long, it is important to pack as much into the time as possible.

Is it necessary to complete one set of exercises on a piece of apparatus before moving on to the next?

No, a good form of training is by using the sequence method whereby you do one set of repetitions at each 'station' in turn and then come back to the beginning and repeat the exercises until you have completed three 'circuits' or sets.

When would I use the Pyramid System, and what exactly is it?

It is a form of training designed to build up strength culminating in a single lift of the maximum possible weight. It is a routine carried out by the more advanced lifters and during the winter months.

It is called the Pyramid System because the number of repetitions reduces until that ultimate weight is lifted. The weight of the barbell is increased after each set.

If, for example you were bench pressing 60 kg in three sets of 10 reps by the end of the summer, you would probably use 40 kg as the starting point of your pyramid and do seven repetitions at that weight. You would then increase the weight to 65 kg, and do six repetitions and so on, increasing the weight each time by 5 kg until you get to a single lift of 70 kg. You would increase your starting point after one week to 45 kg, and so on.

Can weight training be harmful?

It certainly can if you drop a 100 kg barbell on your foot! Most weight training accidents happen not because of the strain put on the body but out of negligence and stupidity. If you have followed the technique guidelines, then you should not encounter problems like slipped discs and muscle strains. And provided you lift within your capabilities without being over-ambitious, or stupid, then you won't be putting any strain on the heart. However, if from a medical point of view, you have any doubts about taking up weight training in the first place, seek medical advice. And to finish, we shall reiterate some important weight training do's and don'ts. If they are adhered to you will enjoy your weight training:

DO:

1 warm up before you start your main training programme.
2 maintain a firm and straight back when lifting. You would if you were lifting a sack of coal. Lifting weights is no different.
3 make sure the same weights are on either end of a barbell.
4 ensure you have a smooth technique. If it is not smooth then invariably you are lifting an excessive weight.
5 remember the golden rule: **NO PAIN – NO GAIN**.
6 however, stop immediately you feel any signs of abnormal pain.

DON'T:

1 run before you can walk. Increase your weights gradually.
2 use equipment that does not have securely fitted weights.
3 attempt bench presses or other strenuous lifts without an accomplice.
4 fool around in the gym.
5 seek advice unless you are prepared to listen to it.

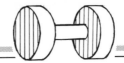

WHERE TO GO

WEIGHT TRAINING

There is a wide range of facilities for weight training right across the country. If you are interested in taking up the sport, take a look at the gym at your nearest sports centre first. These gyms usually have an induction programme which it will be necessary to go through. An instructor will take you around the gym, explaining the machines, how to use them, and what and what not to do with each one. It is then usual for you to register at the gym, pay an annual fee plus a small fee per session.

An alternative to joining a sport centre, is to join a health club. This is a more expensive way of doing things, but it has its advantages. For example, you will be given an initial fitness assessment and from that a fitness programme will be devised to meet your own needs. Your progress – or lack of it! – will then be closely monitored.

Whatever you decide to do, it is essential that you have some form of tuition if you intend to use weights at home. It is all too easy to use the equipment in the wrong way, resulting in considerable damage to your body.

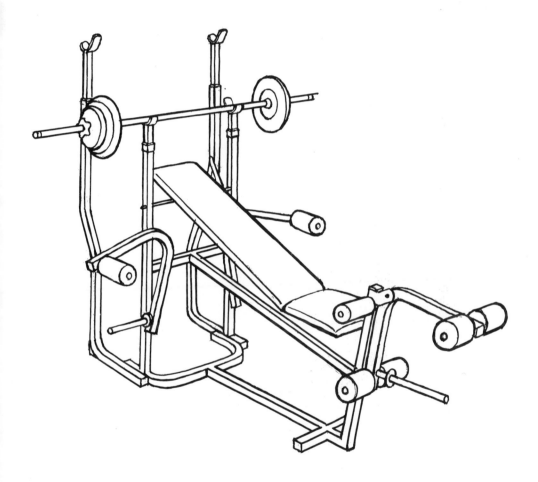

INDEX

PLAY · THE · GAME

Play the Game tells you everything you need
to know, clearly, quickly and simply;

- Expert technical instruction and advice on all aspects
  of the game
- Numerous step-by-step drawings and diagrams
- Unique 'Game Guide' and 'Rules Clinic', to answer
  all your queries
- Tips on the best equipment to use
- Terminology and rules fully explained

Become a winner with **Play the Game**!

ISBN 0-7063-6858-4

9 780706 368581